"There is no other system that balances and connects the human side to the hard side like Metronomics. Its human component sets it apart."

—**LISE LAPOINTE**, former CEO of Terranova Security

"As a result of Metronomics, there is a shared sense of urgency for results within a timeframe or timeline we've specified. It's no longer, 'One day, all this stuff will happen.' Now it's, 'This will happen by this time. We will make it happen.'"

—**ROBERT HAYDOCK**, CEO of AML Oceanographic

"The power of the Metronomics system was that it helped us build structures from which we could tell the story and it was understood by everyone in the enterprise."

—**TRICIA WALLWORK**, CEO of Milo's

The **M** GAME

THE METRONOMICS MONOGRAPH

SHANNON BYRNE SUSKO

METRONOMICS
P R E S S

THE M GAME
The Metronomics Monograph
First Edition

ISBN   978-1-5445-4319-2   *Hardcover*
       978-1-5445-4318-5   *Paperback*
       978-1-5445-4320-8   *Ebook*
       978-1-5445-4321-5   *Audiobook*

To every CEO who is committed to growth but cannot figure out how, this book is dedicated to showing you how to win your M Game every year with ease, speed, and confidence! Let's grow!

CONTENTS

INTRODUCTION

Reflect on the last three years in your business. The last year. The last quarter.

Did you achieve what you said you would in the time you said you would achieve it? Are you confident in the strategy you've set for your company? Is your team clear about this strategy? Is everyone working together and owning their part in executing the strategy?

I'm willing to bet that if you're reading this right now, you've already thought long and hard about the questions posed above, and you've established there is room for improvement.

You are not alone in feeling this way. Most CEOs, in fact, can relate to a lack of clarity around their strategy—for themselves, their teams, and their boards. I myself felt this way at one time.

It leads to wasted time and untimely decisions. You feel like there is no map forward. It's like you push and push and push, but your business just can't get to where you want it to be. You don't gain any momentum.

It's not because you haven't put in the work. You are a learner. You've read every business book you can get your hands on in an effort to become a better leader—from *Good to Great* to *The Five Temptations of a CEO* to the lesser-known titles you often see recommended in your mastermind, Forum, and CEO Roundtable groups and business networks.

And the books are fantastic. Each time you learn a new concept, tool, or framework, you're fired up and ready to implement it in your organization. You roll it out to your leadership team and then the entire company, with a timeline to grow, scale, and achieve success faster. Then you work hard—*really* hard, harder than you ever thought possible—to make it reality.

But you never do. It never catches on. The concept or framework doesn't gain a sustainable foothold in your business. No matter how much time you put in, you can't seem to figure out how to bring those incredible ideas you read about to life.

You put on a brave face. Your ego is on the line. So is your team's trust in you, the company's success, *everything*. But deep down, you know you are losing "your game." You start to think it's a lost cause. Maybe this is just how it's meant to be. What more could you possibly do?

The answer, however, requires you to reframe that question. Whether you're the leader of your first early-stage startup or a seasoned twenty-year Fortune 500 CEO, you know *what* to do. It's *how* to implement the *what* and bring it alive with your team each and every day that is the struggle. You're searching for a playbook that connects your team and your business and that is timely, addressing your goals now but with an eye toward the future, and repeatable so you and your team can turn to it again and again— every day, for that matter—to gain momentum and see the progression.

That's the opposite of what you're currently experiencing. Right now, nothing ever seems to connect. You have a team. You have a plan. But they do not connect in a way that is moving toward your goals.

The same is true of thought leadership. Even though you've read every book the business world has to offer, the ideas are great but siloed. They're not connected.

How do you pull them all together into one connected system that will work for you, your team, and your business? How do you unite every tried-and-true business framework, glue them together, and create and align a repeatable, structured, strategic execution process for your entire enterprise?

The answer is Metronomics.

Metronomics connects your company's team (soft-edge systems) with its business (hard-edge systems) through your established 3 Year Highly Achievable Goal (3HAG), which is your strategy mapped out, quarter by quarter, three years ahead. This forges the critical path to build a foundation for growth, gain momentum, and compound that growth in a stepwise progression. As a result, you achieve what you said you would achieve in the time frame you specified. You have a clear, simple strategy that gives your business a unique and valuable position. And you engage your team to own and execute that strategy using a progressive system.

It's the secret sauce to leveling up your business—finally, in one connected system.

Metronomics was developed based on twenty-plus years of CEOs searching for a system that would create momentum for their business. For many—including myself—success equated to working harder and longer at the expense of one's personal life. Then, my team and I decided something had to change. We couldn't live like this any longer, but we didn't want to give up on our business either. That's how Metronomics was born.

Since its development, Metronomics has been used by thousands of leaders and organizations. In fact, I wrote an entire book titled "Metronomics" on how to implement this progressive growth system. That's right. I added to the repertoire of business texts meant for leaders like you. It contains all the details—everything you need to know—about the only all-in-one system that consistently works. It also tells the story of a fictional CEO named Alex and how embracing Metronomics allowed Alex to become the successful, impactful CEO he'd always sought to be while putting his company on a trajectory for growth.

I know that as a CEO and a leader, you're extremely busy. You might even be resistant to reading yet another business book in fear it won't give you what you need. That's why I've developed this streamlined resource to give you a taste of what Metronomics can do for you and your business. Throughout, you'll hear from CEOs just like you who have used the system to transform their companies—and their lives!

To fully understand and adopt Metronomics, I recommend you read my full book on the topic. But to begin to grasp what the system can do for your company—and for you—read on. See why Metronomics is worth your time and attention. It's not just an execution system or another partial solution aimed at fixing one issue. It's the complete package: a strategy system married with an execution system connected tightly to the team systems—and it's exactly what you've been searching for.

I WAS A DESPERATE CEO

As you continue in this book, you'll read the stories of CEOs and founders who implemented Metronomics to grow up their businesses and finally achieve what they had for so long sought to achieve. My hope is that in reading these stories, you will see bits of yourself in them and see how this system can help you and your team as well.

But before I introduce you to these highly successful CEOs, I have one important story to share: my own.

Believe it or not, I never saw myself as a Desperate CEO— a term I coined for that place we find ourselves when we've read every book and tried every method and still can't get momentum going in our business. But once I developed Metronomics, I saw that I had been exactly that.

My co-founders and I were in our late teens, late twenties, and thirties when we started our first company, Paradata. We had tons of energy, optimism, and drive to bring a new solution to the world. We couldn't have been more excited about our company's global growth potential.

And while we had all that energy and excitement and investors who believed in our future, we had no idea *how* to grow the business up. We started putting in extremely long hours, grinding it out, working harder, like it was a badge of honor to save our egos.

But the extra effort didn't pay off. We spent endless hours working only to not achieve the plan we set out to achieve, disappointing our investors and ourselves. It felt like there weren't enough hours in the day. We were killing ourselves, and for what? Our team trained hard; we worked hard, but we were not winning our game.

Like you've probably done from the moment you became a CEO or leader, I started reading the books of all the most respected and renowned business thought leaders. I attended their workshops and conferences like a rock-band groupie. I took in a ridiculous amount of data and information, hoping to find some kind of repeatable system, a silver bullet, that we could implement to start taking full advantage of our opportunity and achieve the goals our investors expected.

I couldn't find it. There was no one system.

Instead, I found great pieces of systems—disparate and siloed frameworks or tools on specific areas of a business: culture, cohesive teams, hiring, strategy, planning, execution, finance, and cash. They were one-and-done tools that only gave us one perspective at a time, not a connected, sustainable system. In my business, it felt like I was constantly saying, "Look over here and fix this. Now look over there and fix that." It was like a crazy game of whack-a-mole.

That was not going to get me and my co-founders the growth we so badly needed for the company and what we had committed to our investors. So after four years, I went to work with my leadership team and coach to create a system that pulled everything together.

I attended a conference where the creator of the Rockefeller Habits, Verne Harnish, was the master of ceremonies. There, I learned about the One Page Strategic Plan.

Every quarter, we dialed in tactical execution more and more—and learned more together. We knew we needed to go beyond the Execution System we created. We learned about Culture, Cohesion, Human, Strategy, Cash, and Coach Cascade Systems to create seven connected systems known as the Compound Growth System, and now often referred to as the Metronomics Repeatable Playbook. This became our practical and efficient way to grow a company.

It wasn't easy, and it wasn't quick. But over time, we started to see the results of the connected, repeatable system we were building, and step by step, things got easier. We were achieving our priorities and metrics on a weekly, monthly, quarterly, and annual basis aligned to where we wanted to go. We had more clarity and direction and made better, faster decisions. This reduced stress and increased the time spent working on the business, not in the business. The team understood the Core Purpose and actually had a connected system to drive measurable team results. We could see business outcomes grow up quarter after quarter. My board of directors was excited about the clarity and results.

I also began to have more personal freedom in my life, which, at the time, I hadn't even been seeking. Once we began implementing this system, I saw how much freedom I could truly have in my life as a CEO, and I realized just how chaotic things had really been for me and my team. As it turned out, balancing business goals and personal goals was an unanticipated outcome of finding the way to success. But looking back, it makes so much sense.

Eventually, it was clear that we were on to something. We now call that something Metronomics.

When we sold our first company, the company that bought it adopted the system we had developed, and it worked well in an even larger business of four hundred people. We validated the system in my second company from day one by growing up over twelve quarters and then selling the company for an exponential valuation based on our first 3HAG.

The sale of our second company was recognized as one of the top three midmarket deals on Wall Street that year by ACG New York. Afterward, I was contacted by a CEO colleague who had observed our success. He congratulated me for selling two companies in less than six years while complaining that he had been slogging it out for over a decade on his first. He asked if I would consider being his coach.

"I watched you grow up and sell two companies at an unheard-of valuation," he said. "I saw that the second was even more valuable than the first. You must have a system, and I want to implement that system with my team to achieve the same success."

Yes! We did have a system. And I would absolutely share it to allow others to achieve their goals.

That's how I went from Desperate CEO to Repeatable System CEO to Metronomics CEO+Leadership team coach. Since then, Metronomics has spread like wildfire because it works. It worked for me. It's worked for the countless CEOs and leadership teams I've coached. It's worked for the seventy-plus Metronomics CEO+Leadership team coaches we have today from all parts of the world and all of their clients as well.

I *know* it can work for you.

THREE COMPONENTS TO WIN

Think about any winning team you've ever followed. It could be a sports team or a business team. Perhaps you thought of the Chicago Bulls or Los Angeles Lakers, two professional basketball teams who executed the triangle offense, a strategy masterminded by coach Phil Jackson. Or, in business, Toyota, with its Toyota Production System, or Disney and the Disney Way. Both wildly successful companies and their frameworks have gone on to serve as models for corporations all over the world. In every one of these instances, the winning team has three things: a playbook, a scoreboard, and a coach.

WE BELIEVE

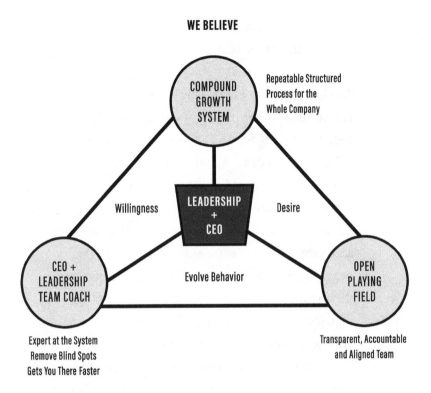

Metronomics is based on the same principles that power those winning teams. At its core, Metronomics is a system that teams—companies—use to *win*. As such, it is broken into three components that reflect a winning team's formula:

1. **A Repeatable Playbook.** This is a repeatable, structured process that actively balances the progression of a highly cohesive team with

alignment and commitment to an organizational plan for the whole team.

2. **An Open Playing Field.** This is where the team can see each other playing the game, working together, asking for and giving help, and making things happen toward their common team goal. In the business world, this is hard to re-create—especially in our hybrid work environments. We have created a virtual playing field, a Metronomics software platform (*www.metronomics.com*), that every team member accesses daily to connect to their team and their plan, take ownership of the metrics through what we call "widgets"—which are the non-fiscal things that flow through your business that the team controls—manage priorities, and forecast and track progress. The Open Playing Field allows the whole team to own the strategy, forecast the win and measure results, or "know the score." Knowing the score is key to any team winning the game.

3. **An expert CEO+Leadership team coach.** This coach understands the playing field and the system to ensure the team is high performing while remaining connected and aligned to the plan. The

coach removes blind spots and unlocks ease, speed, and confidence in the team and the plan to reach your goals sooner.

These three components are fundamental to understanding how Metronomics works for your organization, so let's dig deeper into each one.

REPEATABLE, STRUCTURED PROCESS: THE PLAYBOOK

The Metronomics Repeatable Playbook was developed over many years in my first company and validated in my second. It was then perfected in my coaching practice, both with my own clients and with the clients of other coaches certified in the system.

The Repeatable Playbook comprises seven systems that exist in every business, whether the team is aware of them or not: Cultural System, Cohesive System, Human System, Strategy System, Execution System, Cash System, and Coach Cascade System.

We explain the systems of the Repeatable Playbook as making up a house, as shown in the previous diagram. This diagram has evolved over more than twenty years and represents six of the seven systems in the Repeatable Playbook. It illustrates the balance required to develop and grow a high-performing team to win the game. It provides the regimen to break the process down into practical, progressive steps, each building on the next. It clearly identifies the systems that create a highly cohesive team and the systems that align the team to a differentiated strategic plan to be executed. The result is a high-performing business team that achieves its goals consistently and with confidence.

METRONOMICS REPEATABLE PLAYBOOK

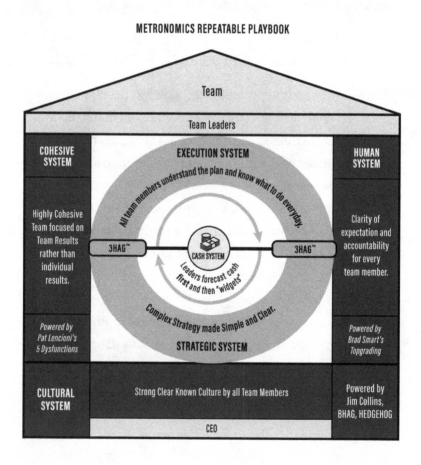

The structure of the house is made up of the three systems that create a highly cohesive, culturally strong team: the Cultural System, the Cohesive System, and the Human System. These systems form the foundation and the frame of the house and are known as the soft-edge systems. They represent the strength of the team and the ability to achieve the plan.

The CEO is the ultimate foundation of the organization, with the team leaders and team members at the top of the house. The stronger the foundation and frame of the house, the easier it will be to execute and achieve the plan aligned with the systems found inside the house, the hard-edge systems—the Strategy System, the Execution System, and the Cash System. The faster that alignment happens, the more rapidly the organization will grow. If any one of these soft-edge systems is missing or underperforming, it will hinder the team's development and put their ability to achieve the plan in jeopardy.

In other words, a business's hard-edge systems are only as good as the soft-edge systems. We can develop the greatest strategy, execution plan, and fiscal forecast but still miss our goals every month, quarter, and year unless the soft-edge systems are in place. But if we maintain a great balance between the soft-edge systems and the hard-edge systems, we will have a high-performing team that is highly cohesive and connected, aligned to the plan, and achieving their goals.

There's more to know about these specific systems, which we'll dig into in a moment, but for now, the key to remember is that the Repeatable Playbook is the nucleus of every company. A conscious, disciplined awareness of this connected system is key to business success. It enables a highly cohesive team and connects it to the plan required to achieve goals. The great news is that no matter where your team is right now, this system will meet you there and build forward.

This core system allows you and your leaders to leverage all those great ideas you gleaned from various thought leaders and plug the principles, knowledge, and tools you want to use into the Repeatable Playbook and connect them. You don't have to choose any one thought leader; you can plug in different tools as your company progresses.

Most thought leaders' tools provide us with a specialized outcome or a view specific to one of the systems, and they can be plugged into the respective system as needed. This diagram shows some of the thought leaders' tools and frameworks that have influenced and can be used within the core system.

We were ferocious learners and consumers of business books while we created the Repeatable Playbook, and we developed a core system that provides a dynamic, practical way to progress and evolve, including plugging in these tools.

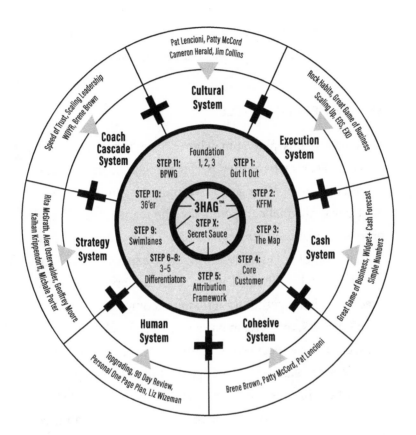

It's always an *and*, not an *or*, when it comes to crafting your playbook. The work of each expert thought leader can easily plug into the system wherever it relates. It will provide a validation of the current state of the company—and a connected, rather than ad hoc, way to grow.

The great thing about this plug-and-play is that the system and your company will continue to evolve with the latest, greatest thought leadership. That's been happening to me and my teams for more than twenty years.

AN OPEN PLAYING FIELD

All sports teams play somewhere: a field, a court, or an ice rink. That's where they perform together to achieve a shared team goal. That goal is winning the game by leveraging their individual competencies, the team's systems and processes, and their strategized plays. Every team has a culture, a level of cohesiveness, and clear expectations of the positions each individual plays. They understand how to execute a plan together for a team outcome.

In business, too, a team has a culture, a level of cohesiveness, clarity of expectations, clarity of roles, a strategy, and an execution plan to win their game. But the playing field—or court or rink—is not always clear or open.

In my first company, the Open Playing Field was captured in the One-Page Strategic Plan from Verne Harnish's *Mastering the Rockefeller Habits* execution framework. It was two pages printed onto one in Word. We outlined the company plan in this format and then shared it through the hundreds of team members throughout the company, every quarter and year, evolving the one-page format over time to reflect a practical and efficient playing field. Everyone had the same plan, except the last column reflected their own priorities aligned to the team plan and goals. This was a huge effort to create an accountable Open Playing Field using paper.

As technology evolved, we tried different project management and business-tracking software. The software didn't create the open, real-time playing field we were yearning for, however, so we went back to the Word version. All the project management and business software we tried removed visible, active ownership behavior from each team member. It didn't connect the individual plan easily to the whole company. The connection and visibility of playing the game together got lost. The behavioral accountability of a team was lost.

At least with the Word version, I (as CEO) and the whole company all had clear visibility of the company plan, and everyone had their own priorities and metrics aligned to the company priorities and metrics.

It was simple but impactful. And we knew it could be so much more.

When I became a coach, I did not want my first clients to have to put in the same effort we had into a Word-formatted Open Playing Field. I wanted them to be able to easily create an Open Playing Field for their team. Those early clients tried many virtual playing fields, but over time, each team slowly moved back off whatever software they chose and back to Word.

I knew Word *could* work, but I also knew there must be an easier way.

I decided to build an Open Playing Field just for my clients because it was necessary to help them grow.

I engaged my friend Benoit Bourget, one of my longtime team members for the last twenty years, to build the platform we had always wanted in our businesses but had previously been too focused to develop. Benoit launched a minimum viable platform for my clients at the end of 2015. I was very careful in stepping my clients into this virtual platform, and their feedback was key to growing the Open Playing Field.

Soon, other business coaches saw or heard of the platform and wanted to use it themselves. I refused. It was only for my clients! But they would not take no for an answer, so Benoit and I founded Metronome Growth Systems—also known as Metronome Software (*www.metronomics. com*)—to offer the Open Playing Field to all companies and coaches who wanted the experience.

The Open Playing Field is a behavioral accountability platform that allows every team member to clearly see others playing the game: their functional roles, their execution, what they are accountable for, their Scorecards, and how they will be measured in the context of the company's priorities and forecasted metrics.

The Open Playing Field shows the team how the game is being played. It creates visibility so that team members can collaborate as they would if they were playing a game together on a field, court, or ice rink. It also provides a way for team members to easily ask for help if they can see they may not achieve what needs to be done to win the game for the team.

The Open Playing Field is one of the keys to developing a high-performing team's transparent and accountable team behavior. For a sports team, the playing field is easy to use to play together; in business, this open field is harder to create to achieve the same execution focus and accountability.

The Open Playing Field mimics the sports environment to ensure the behavior required for each individual to easily commit to a team goal and stay focused on it. The Metronomics Software contains widgets, which are non-fiscal things that flow through your business that a team member owns. This is how your team members are accountable to each other for metrics they own that map to the larger team plan and strategy. It's how they forecast and track progress and work together. It allows leaders to easily coach their team members. And it allows the CEO+Leadership team coach clear visibility of the field on which the team is executing to reach their goals. A high-performing business team absolutely needs an Open Playing Field.

COACH (THE BLIND-SPOT REMOVER)

As a CEO+Leadership team coach, I am a blind-spot remover for the team on the Open Playing Field. It was only when I started writing the *Metronomics* book that I realized that's what I do.

I consistently work with CEO+Leadership teams to help them see what they cannot see because I am observing the team executing from a different perspective.

The Repeatable Playbook and the Open Playing Field help me ask the most impactful questions at the right time. That's why I have learned to trust the system. It guides me to ask the questions needed exactly when my client needs to answer them to remove their blind spots.

In my own leadership journey, I relied on my own blind-spot removers. My coaches started out just coaching me as the CEO, but as time passed, I realized that I needed a coach who would work with me *and* my leadership team together. To be great, we needed to be coached together and to learn together.

No team goes to the Olympics without a coach for the whole team, so why would you and your team go to your business Olympics without a CEO+Leadership team coach?

Of course, you *can* learn and implement Metronomics on your own without anything more than your and your team's willingness and desire to evolve your behavior. You can read, my third book, *Metronomics* and follow the steps and the system. It's very human and organic! With that book, you'll have what you need to create and sustain real forward momentum and growth in your business right now.

Right from the start. But the guidance of a coach will get you there faster, minimizing your time and maximizing your value. What we have observed is that it is three times faster than their peers who are not using the system. You will spend, less time and less investment, by helping you connect your team's behaviors and your confident strategic business goals.

A CEO+Leadership team coach is not a life coach. They are not an executive coach. They are not a CEO-only coach. They coach the whole team together. They are a business team coach. The CEO+Leadership team coach leads the quarterly and annual "practices"—the strategic planning sessions—and coaches the team on the whole system to ensure the plan is solid and aligned while also ensuring that the team implements the progressive regimen required, quarter over quarter, so the company grows with ease, speed, and confidence.

PART 1

SOFT-EDGE SYSTEMS

Now that we've laid out the three components of Metronomics—the Repeatable Playbook, the Open Playing Field, and the CEO+Leadership team coach—let's dive even deeper.

The Metronomics systems sit at the core of the Repeatable Playbook and how the three components work to grow your business up. The soft-edge systems—the Cultural System, the Cohesive System, and the Human System—frame the house and, ironically, provide a clear, solid structure for all teams to achieve their goals. These three systems are present in every company. It's up to leaders to be aware of them and to have the discipline to implement and grow them.

METRONOMICS REPEATABLE PLAYBOOK

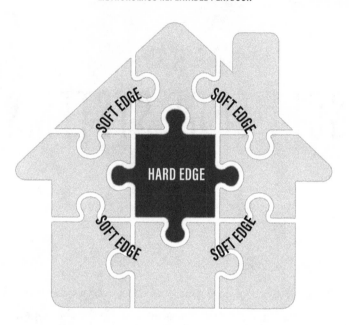

The strength of the soft-edge systems determines the strength of the team—its ability to win the game. They work intensively together and with the hard-edge systems, but it doesn't matter what goes on inside the house if the soft-edge systems aren't functioning well.

Soft-edge systems are foundational for any type of team, whether it be a professional sports team, a beer-league hockey team, a U8 soccer team, or a business team. Without the Cohesive System, we will lose team members. Without the Human System giving clarity of expectations to every team member and keeping them connected to the company goals, we will lose team members. And without the Cultural System, the foundation, the team will not reach its true potential and will quite possibly come to a halt or fall apart.

A more detailed review of each soft-edge system will allow you to further understand their context within Metronomics.

THE CULTURAL
SYSTEM

The Cultural System ensures there is a clear, known culture that creates the team's strong belief in the Core Purpose, team behavioral core values, and the very long-term 10–30 year goal for the organization. It's the necessary foundation of all high-performing teams.

The deep learning and experience behind this system come not only from great thought leaders like Jim Collins and Pat Lencioni but also from the experience of using their principles and those of other thought leaders to create a daily, repeatable behavioral system. This ensures that a company's culture is not something static on paper or up on the wall but something that pulses in the organization every day, starting with the CEO.

ROBERT HAYDOCK
CEO OF AML OCEANOGRAPHIC

I didn't seek out Metronomics or Shannon's coaching for the same reasons many other CEOs do—I wasn't the tired, overworked, overwhelmed CEO who was having trouble managing a personal life along with a business. I was most concerned about—and frustrated with—growth. I didn't necessarily anticipate the impact the Cultural System and people-related aspects of Metronomics would have on our business.

But one of the first things we learned when we began working with Shannon was the need to achieve an adequate level of cohesiveness to foster growth. This required us to focus more heavily on culture, our people, and establishing and clarifying our values. We had to create enough discomfort in the organization to signal that things were changing and that if you weren't on board, you shouldn't be here. We were severing our connection to the status quo.

It took time—probably the first three years of our journey—for me to get comfortable with that, too, and to realize that all the right things to do to push us forward were exactly the things I didn't want to do. But as the CEO, I had to make the first move and have the courage to be vulnerable and step into an environment with which I wasn't familiar.

As a result, the positive, cultural impact has been immense.

Today in our organization, I truly enjoy the people I work with—every single one of them. There are no workplace politics or drama; we genuinely have fun at work and laugh often. It's incredibly engaging and motivating to like the people you work with. That's very much attributed to revealing our Core Values and being relentless in recruiting for those Core Values. The few instances of drama we've had since implementing Metronomics are the direct result of hiring missteps that we made.

I feel a rush when people come to or go from our organization and tell me how this is the most amazing work environment they have ever been a part of—and I know they aren't blowing smoke; those are heartfelt comments. It's very exciting to see people I've worked with grow, knowing that their time at our company put them on a path toward better.

2

THE COHESIVE SYSTEM

The Cohesive System is a practical system that is highly interconnected with the Cultural System to ensure that team cohesiveness progresses and evolves every day in an organization, not just at an off-site two days per year. The Cohesive System is developed through knowing that the daily behavior of the team members will affect the team's level of cohesiveness as a whole. It's difficult to develop a cohesive team while growing a company. It takes time, discipline, and focus.

There is an abundance of great thought leadership in this area. We found Pat Lencioni's *The Five Dysfunctions of a Team* framework to be the most practical in growing cohesiveness, both in our organization and for our clients. As with all the systems, the ideas of various thought leaders can be plugged into each specialty area, helping us to evolve and progress as required.

What I love about Pat's framework is that leaders can implement it and progress with overcoming the five dysfunctions every day, working on team trust, healthy team conflict, team commitment, team accountability, and team results. This provides a great connection to the everyday execution of the hard-edge systems of Strategy, Execution, and Cash.

Every winning team is highly cohesive and works at this together every day. The team holds the reputation of the business in the marketplace in their hands. Everything that happens in the marketplace to serve the customer needs to be shared in a strong feedback system throughout the company. For this to work well, the cohesiveness of the team needs to be high so that team members feel confident in and committed to sharing their feedback.

PATRICIA WALLWORK
CEO OF MILO'S TEA

Overall, our ability to win has come down to one thing: the cohesiveness of our people. Having the right people in the right places doing the right things every day when they come into work is the single most important piece to our growth. Why? Because people equal the behavior in your company, and the behavior equals results.

Our ability to achieve this level of cohesiveness didn't happen overnight, however.

The first day of our two-day Kick Off, when our leadership team tried to articulate our Core Purpose, we couldn't agree. We were talking in circles, debating facts. I knew we had a problem—we didn't have the right people at the table. Without that, we couldn't achieve the level of cohesiveness required to have a productive conversation about these critical elements.

Getting the right people at the table would come to be the biggest part of our Metronomics journey, and it took time to get it right. It took us years to establish our first 3HAG largely because of it. Today, every person on our leadership team who was at the table with me during that two-day Kick Off is no longer at my table. Some of those individuals were instrumental in getting us started, but as we grew and scaled, I was honest with them, and they were honest with themselves. Some are now serving in other areas of our enterprise. Others are being remarkable elsewhere.

As a high-growth company, the Cohesive System— and ensuring we have the right team members at the table and aligned—is a constant conversation. We are always providing feedback through group meetings and peer one-on-ones to ensure everyone understands who we are and who we want to be. For a cohesive team, Metronomics provides the disciplined structure to live the strategy and keep it top of mind and out in front of every single person every day.

ROBERT HAYDOCK
CEO OF AML OCEANOGRAPHIC

Once we wrapped our heads around the Cultural System of Metronomics and built our team based on our Core Values, we were able to have cohesive conversations as a group about tools and processes to figure out what we needed to do to accelerate our growth. For example, we realized we were so focused on macro tools that we forgot about mastering the detailed day-to-day execution as well. Sometimes, the solution is simpler than you think—you may just need the right spreadsheet to make sure you buy the right parts!

As we engaged in these conversations, our cohesiveness advanced, and the benefits of that became apparent.

First, a degree of impatience blossomed within our organization. A shared sense of urgency for results exists that wasn't there before. We no longer talk about our goals in terms of "one day" and instead aim to make things happen within the time frame or timeline we've specified.

There is also an impatience for action. When something goes wrong and there is a lesson to be learned, there is now an expectation that those learnings will be applied in real time rather than slowly or in the future.

In addition, ownership has increased. While I didn't seek out Metronomics because I felt like an overloaded CEO, prior to our adoption of this system, I was incredibly involved in all the details of the company. Just about every decision came through me at the start. Over the last eight to ten years, that has changed tremendously. Now, I have very little to do with the day-to-day operations of the business, such as parts scheduling or engineering decisions. That is owned by others, which has been a huge win for our organization and for me, personally. Full disclosure: I take a lot of vacations. And I enjoy them.

3

THE HUMAN SYSTEM

The Human System was developed and named in my first company after we read Pat Lencioni's book *The Four Obsessions of an Extraordinary Executive*. I wish we had come up with a better name, but funnily enough, this was the name that Pat Lencioni coined, and everything about the system is human. Its purpose is to ensure that each and every team member is supported with the same repeatable process, from recruiting to hiring, to onboarding and training, to clarity of their functional role's Scorecard, to coaching, feedback, and opportunity for growth and rewards.

The Human System ensures that all functional roles the team requires to win are consistently filled with A-Players. A-Players are team members who want to be coached and given the opportunity to grow. A-Players ooze the company's Core Values and consistently exceed performance expectations; they're attracted to being measured and held accountable for the position they volunteered to own on behalf of the team in the company.

The Human System was founded upon Brad Smart's Topgrading methodology and hiring scorecard, which ensures that you hire A-Players nine out of ten times by using a Scorecard that attracts top talent who want to understand what is expected of them through metrics and clear accountabilities. We have been using a practical version of the Topgrading methodology with great success since Brad released his first book. We've found that once you have a team of A-Players, you must have a practical, efficient, repeatable system to support them because they want to be coached, kept, and grown into the next opportunity. And we want to ensure they remain on our team for their next growth opportunity.

The Human System is highly dependent on the Cultural System, as all team members must behave according to the Core Values most of the time, ensuring the culture remains strong. We have also learned that A-Players attract A-Players. These are the team members we develop into a highly

nection to the Cohe-
)erforming team.
) the hard-edge sys-
.ation is functionally
.id execution growth for

JOE MILLER
CEO OF SEAL MASTERS

After about fifteen years of owning and operating a business, I felt like I had taken it as far as I could. I felt stuck.
And as a company, I feared we were about to implode.
Despite trying several models from thought leaders, we
didn't have a system or structure that everyone knew
and understood and that aligned with our execution
plan. We lacked continuity between all business areas
and a solid training platform, as well as a culture that
was more than a gimmick.

I worried all these "stucks" were affecting my ability to attract and retain the best talent. Turnover was
becoming an issue. I would hire a great COO, for example, and then lose them because I didn't have an exciting
plan they could plug into and grow.

Eventually, I realized I needed a coach. That's how
our Metronomics journey began.

The first year was so exciting! We ha[...]
coach, and she had this vast system. We [...]
really ambitious with eight priorities (too ma[...]
ten to twelve people involved in our quarterly se[...]
(also too many).

But there was also, for the first time, a genuine eag[...]
ness throughout the company to succeed in this sys[...]
tem. Upper management was excited that I, as the CEO,
had humbled myself to say to the company, "I need help.
We need help. I don't have all the answers."

As a result, a unique culture began to form. Employees
became invested in the company because they saw
we were doing something super cool. We were doing
something other businesses were not doing—and they
wanted to be a part of it.

By years two and three in this system, our initial excitement settled, and we really began to focus our efforts.

To start, Shannon taught us how to create a proper
functional organizational chart, and once we did that,
it became very obvious who should be involved in our
quarterly sessions. There was a core group of six leaders who would be responsible for executing the plan
we put in place. Yes, these leaders would gather information from people further out to generate that plan,
but this core leadership group would be the ones to
ultimately create the plan and lead its execution.

Once we made that change, we were able to articulate and identify a solid 3HAG. We gained clarity on
who our C-Players, B-Players, and A-Players were, and
we put efforts toward supporting B-Players to become
A-Players and replacing C-Players with A-Players as
quickly as possible.

Today, it feels like much of my job as the CEO is done.
Everyone knows their tasks and their role, and is being
held accountable on a weekly and daily basis in a way
that's visible to everyone and brings them great pride
to show their progress and accomplishments. Now,
I just get to watch it play out and ensure barriers are
removed so the team can progress on their priorities.

PART 2

HARD-EDGE SYSTEMS

Inside the house are the Strategic System, the Execution System, and the Cash System. These hard-edge systems are easy to focus on and define because they have to do with strategy, execution plans, and financial and cash forecasts—hard results. These important systems depend on successful goal attainment. A highly cohesive team itself will not guarantee success. It's possible for individuals to feel connected to other team members and yet still be completely detached from the organizational plans and goals.

Most companies only focus on these hard-edge systems, or at least on two of them. The Cash System is where every company starts—no cash, no company—and the Execution System must work well with the Cash System to sustain itself and grow up the company.

The hard-edge systems are the key to building a high-performing winning team. You cannot win without a confident strategy, clear objectives and goals, aligned metrics, continuous learning, decision-making awareness, team rewards, and an Open Playing Field. Each one of these elements needs to be in place with a highly cohesive team for the team to grow up as a high-performing team that wins every time.

Let's review the hard-edge systems.

4

THE STRATEGY
SYSTEM

lthough business experts include strategy among the hard-edge systems, it can be quite abstract for most companies. Most leaders don't have the same understanding of what strategy is, and many find it a challenge to confidently articulate their strategy.

In Metronomics, the Strategy System's purpose is to take a complex strategy that can be hard for the whole team to understand—even the leaders—and create a clear, simple, understandable strategy the whole team can explain and use to make decisions. The Strategy System, like the other systems, is a progression that ensures the leadership team collaborates to create the most differentiated, confident strategy for their business.

The level of cohesiveness of the team is important to create the most impactful strategy. The more trust there is within the team, the more the team will have a healthy conflictive discussion to decide on the strategy for their business collaboratively.

The Strategy System is made up of the core components and key sequential steps you need to create a confident, differentiated strategy and, most importantly, to ensure that it stays aligned through active knowledge of the dynamics of your market as well as the internal operation of the company. The Strategy System keeps the company in a unique and valuable position, making sure its set of differentiating activities remains relevant and appealing to Core Customers in an evolving market.

As with all the other systems, the Strategy System is founded on the principles of strategy experts such as Michael Porter, Kaihan Krippendorff, Rita McGrath, and Alex Osterwalder, to name a few. The system connects their principles and a few we created into a paint-by-number sequential system and brings them alive. There is no other practical collaborative strategy creation process like it.

The key difference in how a strategy is created through the Metronomics Repeatable Playbook is the prescriptive step-by-step method that allows a whole team to build up their strategy together and validate it every step of the way, creating and maintaining confidence. The entire leadership team is involved, and the team has clarity through the leverage of "strategic pictures" that are created to ensure clarity, focus, and an easy and efficient way to evolve strategy and keep it alive in the company every day.

The foundation of the Strategy system and the glue that holds the Metronomics Repeatable Playbook together is the 3HAG. This is the steppingstone, the evolution vehicle, that connects the strategic execution plan to your cohesive and culturally strong team.

My team and I discovered that if you gut out where you will be in three years' time, as humans, you will never stop validating it to make sure it's right and accurate, thus driving the team to stay immensely focused on the strategy to achieve the goals. And when you align the soft-edge systems with this, the balance provides a consistent way to win each and every year.

My second book, *3HAG Way*, provides a step-by-step, prescriptive method of how to create your 3HAG in great detail. In *Metronomics*, I also cover the progression of the 3HAG and the Strategy System because it is one of the key reasons teams consistently win using Metronomics. The 3HAG is the "goose that lays the golden eggs," as we used to say on our teams. It's the glue that holds it all together.

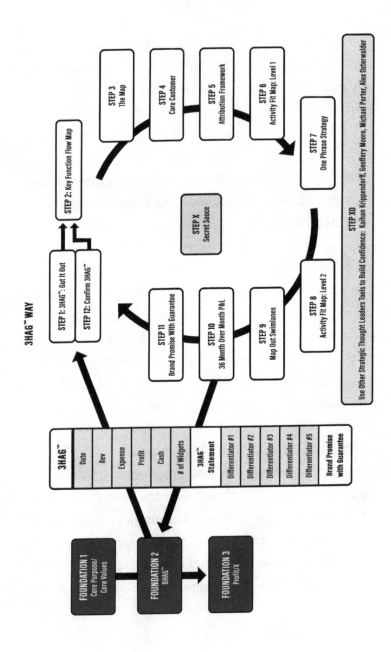

CARL SAUNDERS

FORMER CEO OF VORUM

I was a "stuck" CEO when I found myself literally begging for Shannon's help to implement Metronomics in my company. For years at Vorum, we had maintained the status quo but failed to achieve the substantial growth I was looking for.

After our two-day Kick Off and starting regular coaching sessions with Shannon, there were some massive shifts I noticed right out of the gate.

The first was goal setting. I am a person who delivers on my commitments. Being specific about what we would achieve in years two and three of this system made me incredibly uncomfortable. What if we didn't hit it? What if we didn't do what we said we were going to do?

The incredible thing is we *did* do what we said we would. We achieved the first goal we set and not because we were able to map out discretely exactly what we were going to do to get there but because we had people on the team who were committed to getting there. Come hell or high water, we'd figure it out. That was when I realized that when you have A-Players on your team, they'll do everything they possibly can to get you where you say you are going. And if you don't have the right people in the right seats, those issues outrank strategy every time.

As we progressed in our journey, the concept of setting goals via 3HAGs and achieving them became even more paramount throughout our organization. In fact, hitting a 3HAG of $10 million in revenue resulted in one of the ultimate rewards—taking the entire company to Hawaii!

The fiscal benefits of hitting this goal were obvious, but I could never have anticipated the cultural implications. It lit a fire under our company and unlocked our thinking in unprecedented ways. Everything clicked after that, and our growth took off. We added more A-players to our team and became even more specific with our goals and forecasting.

We dug further into our strategy by identifying who our core customers were and more clearly articulated how we were meeting their needs. We even made headway on creating a brand promise, which is something none of our competitors would ever dream of doing.

Each quarter, we would just keep pounding on our strategy, which got more compelling as our cohesiveness enhanced and our team came together with aligned thinking about the market and how to differentiate ourselves.

While Metronomics helped launch Vorum on a high-growth trajectory, it also was instrumental in achieving another strategic priority with great success: my CEO exit and the sale of our company. With this system in place, my transition out was accomplished in six months, rather than two years, because I was no longer involved in the execution of the company. Our use of the Open Playing Field Software (Metronomics Software) was also essential for showing predictable historical performance, which helped immensely for the company's valuation.

These days, I am privileged to help others on their growth journeys as a Metronomics coach, and I can tell you based on my experience and those of my clients, it is one of the best strategic moves you can make.

What other way is there? Without a system like Metronomics, you'll continue to bump along as you have been. If your company isn't growing, your best people aren't growing or getting new opportunities, and they won't stay. At some point, you need a strategy for growth. And there's no better method for growth than the Metronomics system.

5

THE EXECUTION SYSTEM

The Execution System is founded upon principles Jim Collins included in *Beyond Entrepreneurship 2.0*, Verne Harnish's *Mastering the Rockefeller Habits* and Jack Stack's *Great Game of Business*. It is an efficient way to collaborate on the most important metrics and priorities and ensure they are clear, specific, and owned by leaders. These metrics and priorities are measured for the company on the basis of a 1 Year Highly Achievable Goal or annual plan (1HAG) and a Quarterly Highly Achievable Goal (QHAG) or 90 day company plan. Thirteen Week Sprint Lanes for each corporate quarterly priority ensure visibility into every week of the quarter to make better, faster decisions in the moment as required to achieve the company's

QHAG, not at the end of the quarter. The priorities are then aligned through the owners to other individuals on the team who commit and ensure that these priorities are completed before their own individual priorities.

Company prioritization here is critical. Company priorities should lie ahead of individual priorities always. The ownership and accountability of these clear priorities and metrics are vital to the Execution System interacting fully with the other hard-edge systems, but most importantly with the soft-edge systems.

The Open Playing Field software is essential for driving execution. Widgets owned by each team member foster accountability by making sure individual priorities map to company priorities. It's how you get everyone sprinting in the same direction every day.

Remember that Metronomics is a plug-and-play system, and that includes execution systems. Any execution system can be leveraged within Metronomics—you could be using Entrepreneurial Operating System (EOS), Great Game of Business, or Scaling Up, for example. Whichever system you start with, Metronomics can help you evolve it as your organization grows because it will take the discipline you have with execution and connect it to the rest of the systems in Metronomics.

Long-term and short-term goal setting is also critical to execution. When we started our first company, we thought our Execution System just had to be a twelve-month plan. What we discovered instead was that if we created and leveraged a long-term goal, like Jim Collins's 10–30 year goal, and the 3HAG, a 3 year goal, then creating a 12 month company priorities plan with metrics—both fiscal and non-fiscal—highly aligned the team and brought clarity to what they needed to accomplish. Bringing that clarity together with a daily, weekly, monthly, quarterly, and annual focus on the plan with the team ensured that we made better, faster decisions to get us to the outcomes we had set as goals.

JOE MILLER
CEO OF SEAL MASTERS

Having Metronomics in place, and having the system's rhythm and cadence ingrained in our company, became invaluable during the COVID-19 pandemic. Having this system in place during such a scary, uncertain time was incredibly comforting. It allowed us to remain highly productive, even as we suddenly began meeting and working virtually.

It also gave us the ability to quickly shift in new directions and adjust. We knew how to discuss and focus. We were able to look at our entire workflow, assess how the pandemic was affecting each area—from marketing and sales to design and finance—and make the necessary changes to continue our growth. In a time when many companies felt like things were out of their control, we were able to have plans A, B, and C, and we were able to establish priorities that would make sure we succeeded. We remained in control of our growth, our success, our story—the entire time.

The Metronomics Execution System was absolutely instrumental in that because above all else, it keeps us *connected* every day, every week, every month, every quarter.

Quarterly, our executive team meets to ensure all of our "HAGS" are still real and legitimate and what we want. We ensure we are meeting priorities and have the right priorities to move the company to where we want to go.

Monthly, we meet with the executive team and the larger team—everyone, out to the newest employee—to share these priorities.

We hold weekly meetings tied to each priority where updates are shared and we check in on accountability. We're able to look at the Open Playing Field and see in real time where everyone stands with their responsibilities. The Metronomics Software is a must-have, as it is consistently improving and growing in parallel with our growth.

Finally, every team in the company holds a daily huddle where four quick items are discussed: the good news, the must-do, the stuck, and the score—that is, where we are with the metric related to the team's priority.

These huddles have become so ingrained in our people that if we were to suddenly stop fostering huddles companywide, they would live on. I've heard time and again, "I can't function without my daily huddle." Likewise, chaos would ensue if we did without our weekly, monthly, and quarter meetings.

Once you get into this rhythm, it is an unstoppable motion. You would have to make an effort to stop the momentum once it's going.

The further out we went, the faster this momentum got. It started with the executive team, then went out to the management team, then to the project team, the supervisors, the foremen, and, finally, out into the field.

As people became more comfortable with the system's structure, the software, and the rhythm of the meetings, things started moving even more rapidly— every decision made was implemented faster; goals were met more quickly; turning a new direction wasn't such a heavy lift anymore because everyone was in step and in sync.

As CEO, it has afforded me a great deal of comfort, satisfaction, and peace of mind to know that we've set this play in motion. Now, we just execute it.

6

THE CASH SYSTEM

The Cash System is simple: forecast cash first. In fact, forecast how much cash you want in the bank at the end of every month, month over month, for thirty-six months. You don't just forecast it once and you're done. It's a system. You do this every month with the leadership team. The forecast is owned by the whole leadership team, not just the finance team.

The process is to forecast cash first and then forecast the widgets, the non-fiscal things in your business that your team controls. All teams should be able to forecast their functional widgets month over month through the organization before adding the corresponding fiscal assumptions associated with these widgets.

Most organizations just create a fiscal budget and base it only on past history and percentage increase year over year. My great hope is that once you have implemented Metronomics, you will never forecast that way again.

Forecasting widgets is part of the secret sauce of Metronomics. It is the key to an accurate and achievable fiscal forecast. Team members own and control their widgets, directly connecting the team to a very achievable and realistic plan that in turn connects directly to the cash balance required to grow your business. The more the team owns the forecast, both cash and widgets, the more likely the forecast will be highly achievable. The widgets are key to being able to forecast cash accurately every month and to connecting the forecast and the plan to the team.

As with all the systems, the Cash System is a behavioral progression and is worked up with the team quarter over quarter. The initial goal is to create a thirteen-week widget-based forecast, then move to a twelve-month widget-based forecast, and then add twelve more months—and then twelve more months after that. This creates a best practice of a 36 month widget-based rolling forecast that predicts cash in the bank first and that is owned by the leadership team and based on sound assumptions about the widgets that flow through the company—not on wild-ass or frivolous guesses about "percent growth on top-line revenue."

This system creates a plan that is not only realistic but active. Clear owners forecast the widgets they own with the rest of the team over 36 months. They map out the plan together and review and roll it, if necessary, to execute their strategy all the way out to their 3HAG.

DAVE MYERS
CEO OF APEX LEADERS

We began our implementation of Metronomics after I read *3HAG Way*. I felt it was the connection between strategy and the daily execution of strategy that we were missing.

The Kick Off shifted our mindset to embrace the concept of "good enough for now," which would become instrumental in our ability to forecast financial numbers and set our widgets. Adopting this mindset meant abandoning the feeling that everything had to be perfect from the outset when setting our financial goals and instead realizing that we would constantly revisit and make tweaks to these items as we progressed and improved.

This was not easy for us at first—we had long, hard discussions during our Kick Off and our following quarterly meeting about our numbers and gaining clarity about how our widgets lined up with our financials.

Today, however, those widgets have proven to be the most meaningful aspect of the system for us. We use our widgets as a conduit to the financials of the business. They crystallize for us the main activities we need to focus on to meet our goals, and they help us keep score every step of the way.

It's extremely liberating to know we have the critical number defined for each stage of our value creation mousetrap and the scoreboard is indeed accurate. This wasn't always the case. When we looked back on how many new trials we kicked off or how many new clients we signed in a given period, there was always some uncertainty. "Well, we have a signed agreement, but they haven't kicked off." Does that mean we have a new client or not? With each widget well defined, we no longer waste time debating the facts and instead can focus on either identifying the key issue to a problem that we want to solve or identifying new opportunities to provide incremental value to our customers. Now, everyone is playing on the same playing field and playing by the same rules, which brings clarity to our overall operations.

The ability to operate on the Open Playing Field sets Metronomics apart from any other methodology out there. No other tool provides software support to complement its approach. The interactivity of the Open Playing Field is key. Instead of a static view on a spreadsheet updated once per month, the team across all areas of the business is updating widgets in real time, daily. This gives an accurate count of our operations in the software, and everyone on the team has access to the "scoreboard."

The greatest value of the Metronomics Software, from my perspective, is the ability to leverage it at all levels of the business. Metrics that are used in a weekly one-on-one between a manager and a direct report then roll up to a "team view" and are populated in the agenda for that team's weekly meeting. Team metrics roll up for a "department view" leveraged in the weekly department meeting. And department metrics roll up to a "company view" leveraged in my weekly leadership team meeting.

The fact that we must input our numbers makes us much more cognizant of where we are versus where we want to be and enables us to react more quickly when necessary. This is an important distinction from reviewing an autogenerated or canned report on a daily basis. Trust me, when you aren't hitting one of your personal metrics, you feel the pain of entering an underperforming number in the system. Entering the metric into the software forces you to "live" the metric, whether you like it or not!

This clarity has enhanced our team's effectiveness in several ways.

Widget-driven meetings: The software enables our different teams to maintain a metrics-first mentality, particularly in meetings. We now start off each weekly leadership team meeting with a personal icebreaker, quickly followed by a review of looking at the metrics, and this provides us the lens through which we discuss the rest of the agenda items. It is amazing how talented direct reports can be at guiding a conversation away from a metric they are not hitting. And let's face it: no one wants to talk about underperformance in their role. It's human nature. I'm guilty of it myself. However, by having the widget count right there in the agenda, color coded in either red, yellow, or green, there is no hiding. This allows us to focus the conversation on the brightest "reds" and ask ourselves, "What do we need to do differently to get this widget back to green?" The integration of widget counts gives me confidence that we are having the right conversations in these meetings.

Enhanced leadership team collaboration: My two-hour weekly meeting with our leadership team is the most important two hours of my week in the business. These meetings start on time, and everyone comes prepared, having updated their widget counts and other department metrics in advance. Additionally, my colleagues usually have pre-populated the agenda items they would like to discuss during the meeting. And after reviewing the metrics and widget counts, we prioritize the agenda in real time to make sure we are addressing the highest-priority issues. There is a saying that routine sets you free. Our leadership team meetings are very routine. We cover all the different facets of the weekly agenda in a consistent, coherent manner. Everyone knows what to expect. The only parts of the meeting with potential excitement are when colleagues passionately disagree with one another, in a loving manner. And if we are going to have excitement and surprises in our meetings, this is how we want it: in the form of healthy conflict. Indeed, the routine of our meetings in the software has set us free.

Recently, it's become increasingly important to discuss in our meetings what we are hearing in the market. The data our team members bring to the meeting each week related to this is surprising and eye-opening. We never did that before! We get more out of those two hours now than we ever did in the past.

More employee recognition: We now have the ability to enhance our internal praise of colleagues because we can directly tie performance and progress to the widgets and the score. So often in weekly leadership meetings you are in problem-solving mode. It's important to talk about and recognize the exceptional contributions that occurred the previous week by various individuals on our team.

Overall, I can attest that the rhythm of Metronomics sets you free. It creates real consistency in our organization in terms of expectations and how we prioritize the conversations we have and ultimately leads to a more predictable execution of our business.

It gives me immense confidence to be able to see what's going on in all the different parts of the Key Function Flow Map (KFFM) and to know we have the cadence to ensure all aspects of our business are being covered. As a result, my role has turned into less about being an executor-CEO and more a visionary integrator-CEO. I can more easily step away or focus on other aspects of our company and hand off day-to-day management of the leadership team to someone else. Meanwhile, I maintain visibility into every part of our business. The Open Playing Field is always at my fingertips—via my phone, tablet, or desktop—and I love watching the game being played every day.

ROBERT HAYDOCK
CEO OF AML OCEANOGRAPHIC

Prior to implementing Metronomics at AML Oceanographic, we had tried different tactics to grow the top line for profit. And while these methods were innovative and different for our industry, none of them had the impact that we had anticipated. We worked through exercises to decipher how to differentiate ourselves. We knew how to play a different game and how not to go head to head with our competitors. We were doing some really cool stuff! And yet, we didn't get traction.

What were we missing? What weren't we doing?

With the help of Shannon's coaching, we finally had the tools to focus on the right things and make the calls we needed to make. And when we did that, a lot of great things happened. We built the ability to fund some of the big moves that had to be made on the culture and strategy sides. We could afford to hire that amazing resource who could really up the pressure on the rest of the leadership team to perform at a different level. We could also invest in technology or a new supplier that we couldn't have afforded before.

As a result, we finally saw the impact and results I had been searching for, including dramatically rising cash, revenue, and profit that continues to drive our growth.

PART 3

RESULTS

You might be thinking, "Wow, Shannon, if this is what it takes to win, it seems like there is a lot going on all at once." Right?

And I'm not going to lie. There *is* a lot going on—with or without Metronomics—when growing a company.

Metronomics is a balancing act. We've seen so many companies focus on one area over the other area, teeter-tottering back and forth but never able to balance the soft-edge and hard-edge to gain forward momentum. With Metronomics, the soft- and hard-edge systems get zippered together with the 3HAG.

We will need to activate each of these systems together, step by step. We'll turn the dials each quarter to create a pathway to continue to build your team members from where they are into a high-performing team that achieves its goals, and we'll have a lot of fun doing it. It doesn't have to be painful or chaotic or a whirlwind.

The best thing I can tell you is that Metronomics lays out a clear, step-by-step way for you and your team to take advantage of the progressive nature of the Repeatable Playbook to grow your company.

The result? Growth beyond your wildest dreams.

THE COACH CASCADE SYSTEM

One result of successfully implementing Metronomics is activating the seventh system of the Repeatable Playbook: the Coach Cascade System. Think of the Coach Cascade as the rebar that reinforces the whole house. The purpose of the Coach Cascade System is to grow all leaders into coaches themselves and their teams into high-performing teams connected through the corporate plan. This is a key ingredient in the secret sauce that creates exponential momentum in the team's high-growth compounding results. A team and company can only grow as fast as their leaders.

METRONOMICS REPEATABLE PLAYBOOK FRAMEWORK

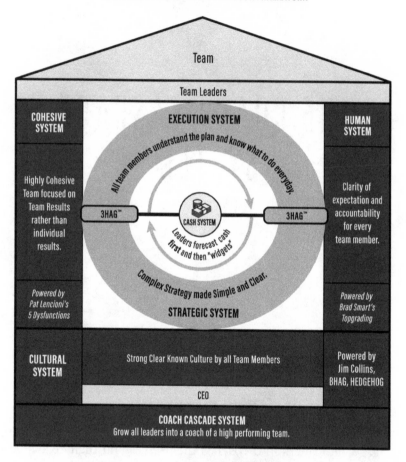

The Coach Cascade System takes the leaders' and the team's behavior to the next level. It takes the team's cohesiveness to the next level of behavior and vulnerability, ensuring that every leader becomes a coach who can create other coaches within the organization—hence the Coach Cascade System.

The Coach Cascade is activated once we've "turned on" the other six systems of the house and have them working well. The system is essential to allowing leaders to grow into "Level 5 Leaders," as Jim Collins has coined it, or what Robert Anderson and William Adams call "Integral Leaders" in their book *Scaling Leadership*. If we don't scale our leaders with the business, we risk stalling out our organization.

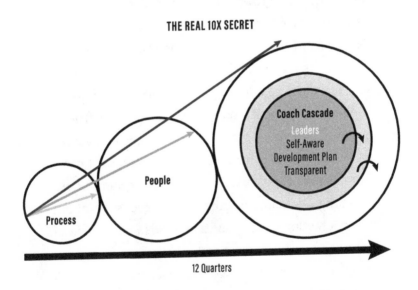

THE REAL 10X SECRET

This Coach Cascade is easiest when you work with an expert CEO+Leadership team coach who coaches the CEO to coach the leaders, and coaches the leaders to coach their own teams, and so on. To grow up our company, we must grow ourselves as CEOs first—and then our leaders and team—into humble coaches with a fierce commitment to the purpose and goal. This is the real 10X Secret to compounding your growth.

PATRICIA WALLWORK
CEO OF MILO'S TEA

Our company's growth has paralleled my own, and I attribute much of that to the Metronomics Coach Cascade. You cannot remain in the role of CEO for a company that's growing this fast without 10Xing yourself. You must be a lifelong learner and be self-aware enough to raise your hand when you need help from a coach or a mentor. I spend a lot of time learning internally and externally from as many channels as I can—from participating in CEO forums to reading books to sitting on boards of other organizations. It's about being intentional with your time inside and outside of your organization to learn and grow.

I think back six years ago; as the leader of our small business, I was involved in *everything*. I touched every part of our business. That was my comfort zone—I'm a good executor. And you do that when you're small. You do what you need to do to keep the doors open.

But you can't grow a business like that. Eventually, you hit an inflection point. You've just spent all these years building your business into what you want it to be. The next step is to give your responsibilities away—pass the football so you can be the inspirational leader for your brand, your associates, and your customers so everyone understands where we're going, what we need to do, and what matters.

The moment I realized this was the moment I knew we had to get an enterprise operating system throughout our organization. You cannot do all the remarkable things that you need to do without it. Today, as CEO, constantly remodeling the operating system is my most important job. It will never be done.

This has required me to unlock my authenticity to all our associates so they can understand the true me and so that I can be in a position to inspire hundreds of people. As the leader of the company and the foundation of the system, it is critical that I inspire our associates, no matter how many we have. The system requires that I transparently share our stories and associates truly see me as accessible and visible. Different CEOs do this differently. Some have a day a month where anyone can meet with them. Others have a group for lunch. There's really no right or wrong way. The point is more to be accessible and real—and relentless in being the Chief

Reminding Officer. I do this through a weekly video for all our associates as well as posting on social media to connect externally with our fans and customers.

Social media is not a comfort zone for me, but it's one example of my growth. It's where I tell stories about our brand, the mistakes I've made, and what I've learned. I've found that's what resonates with readers most—I can stand up all day and say Milo's leaders are authentic, hungry, and agile. But those are just words—the story is what people remember, and the growth I've experienced through the Coach Cascade has fueled me to tell it for our organization.

THE CRITICAL PATH

M etronomics is all about balance—connecting the soft-edge systems to the hard-edge systems through the "score" you want the team to achieve in three years. This is why the "HA" in 3HAG stands for "highly achievable." Your 3HAG is the secret to balancing the soft and hard edges through people—your team—while keeping it all in balance.

To grow up your 3HAG, there is a distinct, critical human path every team follows. The path represents the systems that must be turned on and taken to a certain level to get the results you desire through the three phases of growth in Metronomics: the Foundation Phase to the Momentum Phase through to the Compounding Phase. Teams that experience repeatable and sustainable growth all have followed the same critical path. This makes sense. There is a critical path to "win" your business Olympics. To win your M Game.

Let's dig deeper. To build the Foundation Phase, a team must turn on the Execution, Cash, Human, Cultural, Cohesive, and Strategy Systems. You are probably thinking to yourself, "Shannon, that is six systems—that is a lot!"

THE BALANCING ACT...

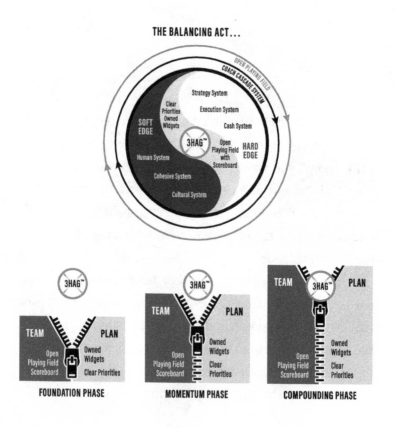

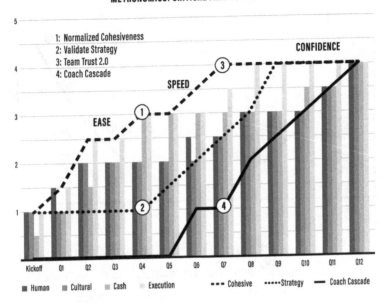

METRONOMICS: CRITICAL PATH TO GROWTH

Agreed. You need to turn them on; however, you only need to bring the Execution and Cash Systems to a level where they are normalized, or working, and the process and rhythm are adopted and a team habit. They are ingrained in the team.

The Cohesive System is at the same level for the leadership team only at this time. This implies and is worth emphasizing that the leadership team must be a 100 percent A-Player team that is at a normalized cohesive level, meaning they have formed and stormed and have now normalized as a team.

STAGES OF TEAM DEVELOPMENT: METRONOMICS TEAM PROGRESSION

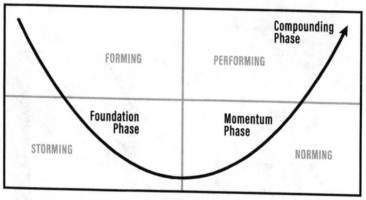

Credit: Bruce Tuckman

They have team trust. They have healthy team conflictive discussions. They are committed and accountable to each other, and they are focused on the team's results rather than their own. This means they have scored more than or equal to 80 percent green and 20 percent yellow in four out of five areas in Pat Lencioni's Five Dysfunctions of a Team Assessment.

The Strategy System is turned on and there must be a strategic rhythm in place for the leadership team, where at minimum the strategy is mapped according to the 3HAG Way's step-by-step mapping process. The strategy is not fully validated, but there is much more clarity for the team than there ever has been. The strategic pictures, which are an outcome of this process, clarify every step for the whole leadership team to tell the same strategic story.

The other two systems that are turned on, not to the same level as Execution, Cash and Cohesive Systems, are the Cultural and the Human Systems. These systems don't need to be at the same level as the others, yet to move through the Foundation Phase to the next phase of growth, the Momentum Phase, these systems must at least be turned on to support the other systems.

The Cultural System must have been discovered through an established core purpose, team core values, and the organization's known 10-30 year goal—their BHAG™, as Jim Collins has coined it. It has to be in a good enough state with known team habits to continuously evolve.

The Human System has clarity of Scorecards for all functional roles that the leaders own. Ninety-day coaching reviews have been established and carried out for the leaders, and the company has a known active widget-based scoreboard through its active Key Function Flow Map (KFFM).

When a company is in this place, the team experiences growth in their fiscal results, but more importantly, the leadership team has more time to work on the business rather than in the business. They have more time to plan, look ahead, coach, and grow their team. They are having fun! They have time to validate their strategy. This is key to unlocking the next phase of continuous sustainable growth and moving to the Momentum Phase.

All of the above must be true to grow from the Foundation Phase to the Momentum Phase. This should help you understand why so many companies stay so long in the Foundation Phase without getting the results they hoped for: they never get out of the forming and storming stage as a team, and they literally give up on their goals and settle with mediocre results. The CEO must be motivated, have the energy, and commit to taking their team and company to the next growth phase.

Committing is bold and rewarding. In my experience, the toughest step in the Foundation Phase for the CEO is not in the Execution, Cash or Strategy Systems, it's in getting a 100 percent A-Player leadership team in place. I have seen this stall companies out and stunt their growth opportunity; they never get out of the Foundation Phase, no matter how great their Strategy, Execution, or Cash System is. They slog along for years—decades, even—before they finally give up on their original vision. This is very sad. Don't let this be you and your team.

Even if you have one person on your leadership team who is not an A-Player, I can confidently say this will make growing your company hard. Very hard indeed. An A-Player leadership team is the key to moving from the Foundation Phase to the Momentum Phase and building the value for your shareholders. If this was a professional sports team, you would put your A-Players on the field to have the best chance to win the game. This is the exact same principle in the sport of business in your M Game.

The Momentum Phase is just that. This is where you and your team will create speed by continuing to evolve and ingrain the Execution, Cash, and Cohesive Systems. You will bring the Cultural and the Human Systems to a similar level through cascading through the whole team. You will bring the Strategy System to a validation level to ensure there is confidence by all in the company's strategy. This is done through the step-by-step 3HAG process and the strategic pictures, making it easy to share the strategy with the whole team. The clarity and confidence the team has allows them to make better and faster decisions every day.

It is hard to validate and share the strategy with the whole team unless the leadership team is 100 percent A-Players who are cohesive at a normalized level. This allows for healthy debate and conflictive discussions to validate the strategy with confidence. If the Execution and Cash Systems are not working, no one will be able to focus on strategy, no matter how cohesive your team is. If your team is not cohesive, there will be no time for strategy as well.

With the Momentum Phase, a team will experience incredible growth of more than 20 percent year over year. This is why you need to commit to all of the above as it makes getting this growth and sustaining it much easier and predictable.

To move from the Momentum Phase to the Compounding Phase, the Strategy System is working well, with the whole team involved in strategy. The team is confident in the strategy and the system to create and validate. The cohesive levels of the leadership team and their teams are beyond normalized, and everyone is connected to the team score. This is known as a team in a high-performing stage. All the other systems are high performing as well (four out of five), except the Coach Cascade System. To move from this phase to the Compounding Phase, the leadership is at a level of cohesiveness that is what we call Team Trust 2.0. This is where the leadership team has a real-time humble and active peer to peer feedback loop in place. The leadership team trust is so high that peer feedback is provided without being prompted. This proves to be a great example for the rest of the team and must be in place to turn up the Coach Cascade System which moves the team into the Compounding Phase.

In the Compounding Phase, because all the other systems are working well, the leaders can now turn up the Coach Cascade System by continuing to grow themselves first and coaching the same growth out to their leaders, and their leaders to their teams. This is where we can only experience compounding growth with ease, speed, and confidence if—and only if—the CEO, their leaders, and their teams have time to grow themselves at the same pace as the company's growth.

This is why we put all these habitual team systems in place. This is what unlocks compounding growth of an A-Player team. The leaders now have time to coach their leaders into becoming coaches as well. The CEO must be willing to grow into what Robert Anderson and William Adams would call an "Integral Leader". Jim Collins would call this type of leader a "Level 5 Leader,"—humble and fiercely committed to the team goal. The rest of the leadership team must be committed to and on this leadership journey as well. This is the only way a team will remain in the Compounding Phase. The Compounding Phase and our experience is well supported with the research and framework found in the book *Scaling Leadership* written by Robert Anderson and William Adams.

This is the critical path to grow your company in a repeatable, sustainable, human way. Metronomics unlocks this through its business operating system and regimen of drawing upon the greatest business thought leaders of our time and ordering their work in a human behavioral critical path that works every time. This is why we plug and play so many thought leaders' tools into Metronomics to drive and keep teams on their critical path of growth.

All teams can assess where they are on the path and can identify what they need to do. (Please take the assessment at *www.themgamebook.com* (secured) to find out where you are on your path and what the next steps should be.) All

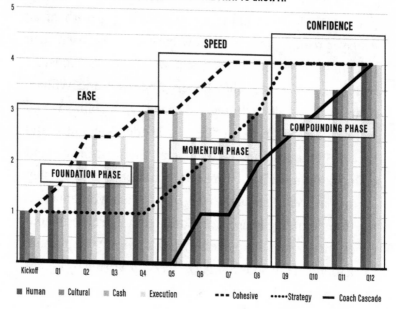

METRONOMICS: CRITICAL PATH TO GROWTH

teams need to do is to commit to their growth through actioning Metronomics. Every CEO interviewed for this book is aware of what growth phase they are currently in and is working with their Metronomics coach and team to grow forward to the next growth phase.

These phases have been around as long as companies have been in business. Our research, work, and experience have unlocked the clarity of how every team can move step by step from phase to phase to reach their goals rather than giving up or settling. Find out what path you are on, and commit to the next steps.

As James Clear said, "You do not rise to the level of your goals. You fall to the level of your systems." Metronomics is all about balancing your systems. It's the only solution out there that ties together the development of a team with the systems of business to guide your team through the Metrononics critical path to drive predictable growth.

The predictable, progressive growth that happens through Metronomics is the result of a process called "team habit stacking." Team habit stacking means every individual on your team commits to displaying the same daily behaviors and habits at the same time and continuously stacking new habits to grow as the company grows. The team is swimming in the same direction, prioritizing the same behaviors, and instilling the same habits.

Team habit stacking is enabled by the Metronomics critical path. As the seven systems stack each quarter, almost like a staircase, it creates that pathway for teams to rise to the level of their systems and achieve the goals you've set.

Daily functions of Metronomics contribute to team habit stacking as well. By logging into the Open Playing Field every day, team members form an agreed-upon habit. Over time, the commitment to this habit contributes to their growth. Of all my clients, the ones that log in to the Open Playing Field daily grow three to five times faster than organizations that log in less frequently. Day after day, week after week, month over month, quarter over quarter, they're stacking and stepping, improving and growing each time. Their focus on where they are going is unwavering.

PATRICIA WALLWORK
CEO OF MILO'S TEA

Having the courage to get clear on the who in our organization was extremely difficult as we grew through the phases of Metronomics. This is particularly the case for Milo's because of the legacy and maturity of our business—there were people who had been on our team for a long time. Making the call that someone wasn't playing along or behaving the way we needed them to was tough, even if it was the right thing to do and we were doing it in the right way.

But what we learned is that having the right people at the table is not a wish or a hope or a dream; it's a truth that is critical to growth. Figuring out who those right people are is part of the Metronomics critical path, and it's unique to every organization. What works in my seventy-six-year-old startup culture isn't going to work in somebody else's.

But if you don't make those hard calls and get A-Players at your table, you will struggle, and your journey will be a lot harder. You need people who are willing to listen and be open to what you're trying to do.

We now have the right people in the right spots, and it not only has skyrocketed our growth, but it is fun! It propelled us into the Compounding Phase, which is where we are today.

I think back to our early days adopting Metronomics and how frustrating it was—I didn't have the right team. I didn't have the A-players. But I can say the struggle of walking that critical path was worth it. Today, I feel gratitude and thankfulness. We've done the work. We have the system and the people. Now, we just keep remodeling and compounding because our growth is never done.

ROBERT HAYDOCK
CEO OF AML OCEANOGRAPHIC

It's common for companies to start out with Metronomics wanting to focus heavily on strategy, but Shannon emphasized keeping the systems in balance and adopting the "good enough" mindset, which is the idea that a system doesn't have to be perfect before we move on to focusing on the next one. Because to move out of the Foundation Phase of Metronomics, we only needed to map our strategy. We also had a few more boxes we needed to check, including normalizing our Cash System by leveling some of our fiscal numbers, having clarity on our Execution System and the KFFM, and normalizing our Cohesive System.

There was also a "ripping off the Band-Aid" moment during this time to truly get the right people on our team. I see now that there were a few key personnel changes that took too long to make, and it held back our growth. Some top-level leaders just didn't understand where we were going. Some individuals only wanted to commit to the status quo.

If there's one thing I've learned about traveling the Metronomics critical path it's that results are directly proportional to your willingness to walk toward what scares you. There is no "safe way" through this system that really works. To reap its incredibly powerful bene-fits, you have to fully dive in, and that often means being honest with yourself and doing things that make you extremely uncomfortable.

WHY METRONOMICS WORKS

O nce organizations discover Metronomics, it transforms their companies, their teams, and their lives. It's taken $3 million companies to an exit for $110 million in less than five years and $100 million companies to $500-plus million in three years. It has contributed to huge growth for companies large and small—mine included.

Metronomics will clearly map your strategy and align your execution, allowing you to spend less time, less effort, and less money to grow your business. To stop grinding. To stop working ridiculous hours and start "winning." Do what you said you would do in the time you said you would do it.

Metronomics will help you get your life back and build the business you always envisioned.

GROWING UP

As CEO, you are the one who must spearhead this effort. Without a CEO who has the willingness and desire to commit to achieving their goals and evolving their behavior, Metronomics won't work.

Metronomics is founded on the CEO+Leadership team's behavior and willingness to commit to the system to grow up their company to achieve their goals while living the life they want. Each individual must be willing to evolve from the leader they are today into a continuously improving version. From Leader 1.0 to Leader 5.0. If they do this, their company will follow—and so will their life.

Just by reading this, you show that you have the desire to grow—to grow yourself, your team, and your company into a high-performing business team that brings together developing cohesiveness connected to the visible elements of the collaborative plan. Now, you just have to put all of that into place.

And while it's simple, it's not easy. I don't think I've ever met a CEO or a leadership team who doesn't want to grow their company. Everyone wants that! But for many people, growing their company is one of the hardest things they've ever faced.

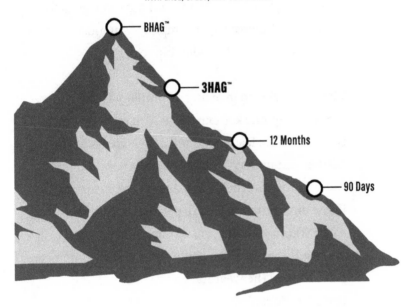

CLIMBING THE MOUNTAIN
WITH EASE, SPEED, AND CONFIDENCE

BHAG™

3HAG™

12 Months

90 Days

Many thought leaders say that growing a company is like climbing a mountain. I have never climbed a real mountain, but I am fascinated by mountaineers and mountain climbing. I've studied many successful climbs—and they are all founded upon the same regimen as Metronomics.

Consider how the barriers to climbing a mountain relate to the barriers of growing a company:

- **The #1 barrier to growth is Leadership.** It sounds harsh, but it's true. You cannot summit a mountain without a strong A-Player and a cohesive, high-performing leadership team, and the same goes for a company. To grow up a company, you must have a 100 percent A-Player leadership team.

- **The #2 barrier to growing a company is the lack of deep market expertise.** You must ensure that the whole leadership team are experts in the market and understands the market well. A team wanting to grow their company must be experts in the environment they're playing in. Just like when you're climbing a real mountain, you don't necessarily control the environment. A mountaineer can't control the weather, and a CEO building a company doesn't control the market.

- **The #3 barrier to growth is lacking the right infrastructure at the right time.** This means when you need it, not too soon or too late. Think of how a team of mountain climbers moves first from base camp and then to camp after camp up the mountain. They move their infrastructure as they climb. It is no different in business. If you know your long-term and near-term goals, it is easier to make infrastructure decisions, now and in the future, to help reach those goals.

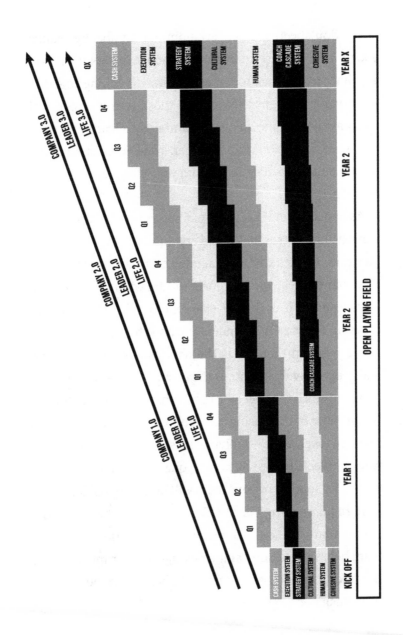

You don't become an expert mountain climber by reading books. You start by finding other mountaineers who want to climb mountains, too, and you start climbing together. You don't go straight to Everest. If that's your ultimate goal, you start with some smaller mountains to learn and grow with your team. You train together. You become better and better, mountain after mountain, year after year. You progress together.

As a CEO and leadership team, growing up a company using Metronomics is very similar. At the heart of Metronomics is a CEO+Leadership team that wants to win. They want to achieve their goals and are willing to learn new ways to make it easier for everyone to win. Metronomics is set up for the CEO, leadership, and the whole company. It is a regimen that meets the team where they are today and progressively promotes the best practices of growing a company until they become habits that will endure through the lifetime of the business. By following the Metronomics regimen over time—evolving in small steps day by day, week by week, month by month, quarter by quarter, year by year—the solidity of your team will be unstoppable.

It requires an inspired CEO leading a cohesive leadership team to make this happen. It takes patience. Human team behavior—team habit stacking—takes time to evolve. But once it begins, we can climb to heights we never could have imagined.

ALIGNED EXECUTION

What's more, Metronomics is a system for all sizes of business in any industry.

So many methods you find in the business books are focused on startups. They aim to help brand-new CEOs take small companies from zero to ten. Metronomics is for all CEOs and leaders, no matter what size the business.

Bigger companies have the same growth challenges as startups. Why? Because there are people involved, and a team of any size requires coaching. In fact, I predominantly coach businesses that are over the $100 million level and far larger. Whatever the size of your business team, you will benefit.

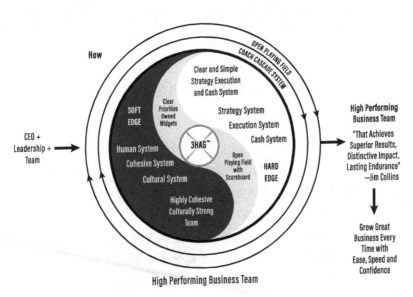

High Performing Business Team

Pulling together all the pieces of business-thought leadership isn't just about the systems. You definitely need a system. But just as important is the team. A team with a clear plan connected to a transparent Open Playing Field with widgets is the backbone that makes Metronomics work—every time!

Metronomics is founded upon vision, connected to strategy, connected to tactics, as Jim Collins eloquently describes in *Beyond Entrepreneurship 2.0*.

Metronomics connects the team and their behavior to the seven systems that exist in every business: Cohesive, Culture, Strategy, Execution, Cash, Human, and Coach Cascade.

Metronomics keeps these systems in balance so you can grow your team, your company, and your life.

PATRICIA WALLWORK
CEO OF MILO'S TEA

When I first began working with Shannon, I remember during our Kick Off feeling optimistic that Metronomics finally could be a system that would work for us.

And without a doubt, *it has* worked.

By dedicating ourselves to this system, we have achieved explosive growth at Milo's. In the six years we have used Metronomics, Milo's has grown by *fivefold*.

The year we started, we sold nine million cases. This year, we'll sell forty-five million. I frame this growth in cases sold because that was our widget, the score by which we measured our progress and success.

I attribute this success to several factors enabled by Metronomics, including the cadence the system offers. Our relentless discipline around the system and refusing to be complacent has been key to our success. At first, the cadence was met with a lot of pushback in our organization. But once we did it and lived it, we saw that you can't *not* have a cadence. It's groundbreaking and essential to the information flow. We could not have navigated our explosive growth without it.

The Metronomics operating system has also been instrumental in helping us create a culture around established expectations and accountability for every person, every leader, to do their functional part.

We found this particularly true during the COVID-19 pandemic, when our culture became a differentiator for us among our competitors. That was the real moment of "Are we who we say we are?" And we not only proved it; we exploded.

We were able to have products on the shelf during the supply chain issues when our competition couldn't. We gained loyalty and strengthened our relationship with our customers because we were available, reliable, and on time. We did what we said we were going to do—and during a global pandemic. That served as rocket fuel for a train that was already on the tracks.

LISE LAPOINTE
FORMER CEO OF TERRANOVA SECURITY

When I first met Shannon and my Metronomics Coach, Damian Byrne, I had been an entrepreneur for thirty-five years and had been CEO of Terranova Security for fifteen. At that time, I found myself at a crossroads: either we needed to grow Terranova Security, or we needed to sell it. I didn't feel like it was the right time to sell.

When I learned about Metronomics, I realized this system was the solution we needed for growth—and it was.

For the next five years after committing to Metronomics, our company achieved 50 to 60 percent growth per year. After those five years, I exited the company at a valuation that met my expectations, but the implementation of Metronomics lives on at Terranova Security because we could not have achieved what we did in that five-year span without it.

When other people ask me how I did it—what my secret to success is—I tell them all about Metronomics. I tell them how disciplined and structured I needed to be because if you as the CEO aren't disciplined and committed to this system, you can't expect anyone else to be. It's common, however, that after telling someone how I achieved what I did, the person goes right back to doing what they were doing.

The reality is that it isn't easy to be committed to this system. It requires the courage to let go of the people who are wrong for your business and to surround yourself with team members who can put ideas on the table in a cohesive and collaborative way in the name of company growth. You also have to let go of the notion that you make all the decisions. That may feel different, but it's also freeing, like a weight is lifted off your shoulders.

Compared to other operating systems, what sets Metronomics apart is its human component. There is no other system that balances and connects the human side to the hard side—the soft edge with the hard edge. It also brought our management team closer together. We had fun, laughed a lot, and found a great deal of happiness working this way.

For me, it relieved a lot of stress as a CEO. I was no longer alone at the top making all the decisions myself. I had a team to collaborate with that understood where we were going. And because of that, we were able to win.

WILL YOU WIN YOUR M GAME?

M Game represents a new beginning of great success, as it is the exact opposite of the end game mentality. Rather than focusing on one single endpoint or goal, the M Game offers an ongoing system of growth and optimization that leads to sustained success aligned to your 10 year, 3HAG (3 Year) and 1HAG (1 Year) goals.

The M Game, also known as the Metronomics Game, offers a comprehensive business operating system that CEOs and leaders can rely on for sustained success. Once you start playing the M Game, there's no need for any other business operating system, as it provides everything you need to win your game, whatever that may be. This strategic approach focuses on creating maximum value in minimum time, ensuring that businesses are sustainable and scalable for the long term. Once you begin playing the M Game, there's no need to stop because it's an infinite game that offers ongoing growth and optimization within the arena you are playing.

The M Game is just the start of your infinite journey in the sport of business. It's not an end game, but rather the beginning of a long-term process that requires a commitment to ongoing learning, development, and improvement. By focusing on maximum value and minimum time, the M Game offers a one united business operating system that emphasizes innovation, creativity, and adaptability for the whole team. Metronomics is the united system that enables businesses to win at the sport of business, by providing a regimen for sustainable growth and success. However, winning in business is a team sport, and it takes a whole team to achieve sustained success with Metronomics.

Metronomics gives you the structure you need to develop a great team that will share your willingness and desire to evolve and grow. Remember, the greatest teams have three things in common:

1. A structured, repeatable process that all team members follow.

2. Clarity of expectations of each other and a willingness to work hard to develop and maintain high cohesiveness to achieve their team goal and score together.

3. A coach who is an expert at the repeatable process and who ensures the team has clarity of role and position while keeping it highly cohesive and focused on the team result.

METRONOMICS: HOW

Metronomics Repeatable Playbook

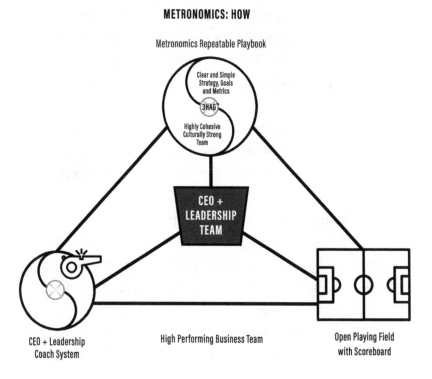

Metronomics provides those critical elements in its three components:

1. A Repeatable Playbook (Compound Growth System)—a systematized, structured approach that combines your team systems with your business systems.

2. An Open Playing Field via an easy-to-use software platform (*www.metronomics.com*) that serves as a known, transparent, accountable, and aligned way for the team to play together. All your team must do is log in to the playing field every day, own their widgets, and know the score, and everyone can win.

3. The guidance of a CEO+Leadership team coach, an expert at the system who ensures that the company and team grow with momentum to reach their goals.

We have studied and evolved high-performing business teams for over twenty years while striving to implement a dynamic business operating system for growth and goal achievement. What we found is that you cannot achieve success without having both in place: a highly cohesive, culturally strong team *connected through a 3HAG* to a clear and simple business (Strategy, Execution, and Cash) system.

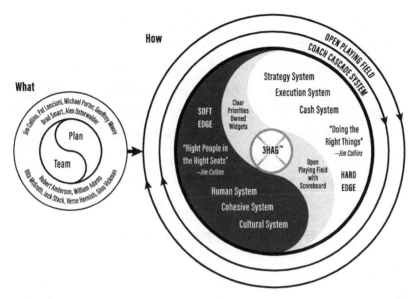

High Performing Business Team

We have taken the what of all the greatest thought leaders and pulled it together into one connected system that shows you how to balance your team (the soft-edge) and your business (the hard edge).

Most CEOs I know run from the words *culture, cohesiveness,* and *human.* Instead, they focus on the business systems: cash, strategy, execution. A focus on the business systems won't make it easy to grow a company over the long term. It needs to be balanced from the beginning with attention to the soft-edge systems and the hard-edge systems. Growing up a company is a true balancing act, and

Metronomics ensures that you and your team get balanced and stay that way as your team habit stack and continue to progress on the Metronomics critical path to success.

There is no other strategic execution system out there that does this for companies—instilling this balance, turning on the systems, and allowing for the ease, speed, and confidence in an organization's growth.

It's truly a secret sauce, right there for you to implement.

METRONOMICS: EASE, SPEED, AND CONFIDENCE

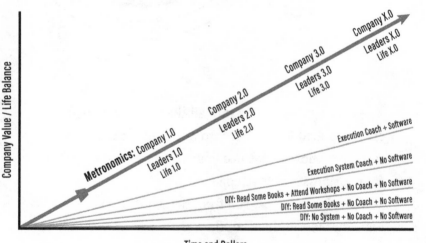

And it works.

It *so* works.

Damn, it works!

I want you to minimize time and money invested and maximize value and life balance while building the company you want. I want you to be able to do what you said you would when you said you would do it. I want you to feel clear and confident in your company's strategy and know your team is also clear and confident and owning their part in your company's strategic execution. I want you to grow up your company in a swift, predictable way. And I want you to see you don't have to sacrifice the life you want to get the company of your dreams—you *can* have both.

I know this works because I lived this system. I won my M Game twice. My clients who lived the system achieved the same results I did. The clients of Metronomics coaches around the world have done the same. They are winning or have won their M Game.

You can win your M Game too.

All you need to do is Kick Off with your team.

ACKNOWLEDGMENTS

I would like to express my gratitude to everyone who helped make this book a reality. First and foremost, I want to thank my husband, Sko, and my children, Cain, Matthew and Embyr-Lee, for your unwavering support and encouragement throughout the writing of this book. I am also deeply grateful to my incredible Metronomics Team and Coaching Community. Your insights, feedback, and encouragement have been invaluable to me, and I couldn't have done this without you.

Thank you to all the CEO+Leadership Teams who have committed to growth utilizing Metronomics. I would also like to extend a special thanks to Carl Saunders, Dave Myers, Joe Miller, Lise Lapointe, Patricia Wallwork, and Robert Haydock, who share my commitment to growth and generously shared their experiences and insights with me. Your perspectives and stories have helped to shape this book and make it a richer resource for leaders. Thank you for your time and wisdom and for your dedication to helping others succeed in their businesses.

I would also like to thank Scribe for your exceptional guidance and expertise. Your keen eye and attention to detail helped to shape this book into its final form, and I am grateful for your support and feedback.

Finally, I want to express my heartfelt thanks to the readers who have picked up this book. Your interest in my work is a true honor, and it is my hope that the insights, strategies, and systems in this book will help you to grow and succeed in your business beyond your wildest dreams. I am deeply grateful for your support and trust, and I hope that this book will provide you with the one united system you need to achieve your goals and reach your full potential.

ABOUT THE AUTHOR

Shannon has more than twenty-five years of experience building and leading high-growth companies. She co-founded, served as CEO for, and led the sale of two companies less than six years apart: Subserveo Inc (founded in 2008 and sold 2011) and Paradata Systems Inc. (founded in 1995 and sold in 2006).

Shannon is a renowned entrepreneur with expertise in consistently linking strategy, execution, and cash with high-performing team coordination to achieve sustained success. She is highly regarded for her ability to lead teams and implement a replicable strategic execution system, which she first created in her own company and later validated in her second company by achieving rapid growth and a successful exit. Shannon now coaches CEOs who aspire to replicate this success using her strategic execution framework, which is known as Metronomics.

In June 2011, Shannon established a business focused on coaching CEOs and leadership teams worldwide. She also co-founded Metronome Growth Systems, which is a cloud-based business platform centered on Metronomics's best practices for high-growth businesses, CEOs, leaders, and business coaches. In July 2018, Shannon founded Metronome United, now known as Metronomics United Coaching, which now has over eighty coaches worldwide who are dedicated to implementing Metronomics business operating systems powered by 3HAG to strategically impact high-growth companies and their teams.

In July 2014, Shannon wrote and released the Amazon bestseller The Metronome Effect: The Journey to Predictable Profit. Her second book, 3HAG Way, was released in April 2018 and was an Amazon bestseller and a 2019 finalist in the International Book Awards. Shannon's latest book, Metronomics, released in June 2021, was #1 on Amazon in Canada, USA, and Australia.

Shannon won the Universal Women's Network "Game Changer" award in 2022. She was recognized as one of Canada's Top 100 Most Powerful Women in 2018, 2020, and 2022 and was awarded Canada's Top 40 under 40 in 2001. She received the Sarah Kirke Award for Canada's Leading Women Entrepreneurs in 2006. Shannon was named Deal Maker of the Year in Vancouver in 2011 and was in the top three midmarket deals on Wall Street that year.

Shannon has Bachelor's degrees in Commerce and Computer Science from Saint Mary's University and a Master's in Computer Science from the Technical University of Nova Scotia. She is married with three children and resides in beautiful Whistler, British Columbia.